BRADWELL'S IMAGES OF

Dorset

BRADWELL
BOOKS

STURMINSTER NEWTON

QUIS METUIT

HEART OF THE BLACKMORE VALE

MEDIEVAL TOWN TWINNED WITH
MONTEBOURG

A TASTE OF DORSET

LYME REGIS · STURMINSTER NEWTON · STAIR HOLE, LULWORTH COVE

Introduction

Step inside Bradwell's Images of Dorset and treat yourself to an enchanting visual feast. Using outstanding technical skills coupled with an absolute love of their subject matter, Susan and Andrew Caffrey have created a collection of images that portray the essence of Dorset in all its depth and variety. From the iconic to the unknown, these photographs will have you itching to return and explore again and again, and perhaps give you some ideas for capturing your own photographs! *Enjoy!*

Durdle Door

Durdle Door is Dorset's world-famous natural limestone arch. From Lulworth Cove, take a boat ride across the calm sea or brave the steep cliff walk to reach the landmark. The unspoiled beach is a great place to bring a picnic, take a dip in the water or sit and enjoy the views.

West Bay

Golden sandstone cliffs and outstanding beaches have earned West Bay the title 'Golden Gateway to the Jurassic Coast'. The lively marina offers fossil-hunting, crabbing, and traditional fish and chips using locally caught fish. Hire a boat and row up the River Brit towards the nearby town of Bridport.

Lyme Regis

Lyme Regis is Dorset's most westerly town and famous for its wealth of fossils. Stroll along the Cobb, a historic stone pier, for fishing and splendid sea views. Enjoy a Dorset cream tea beside the bustling harbour or go fossil hunting along the Jurassic Coast.

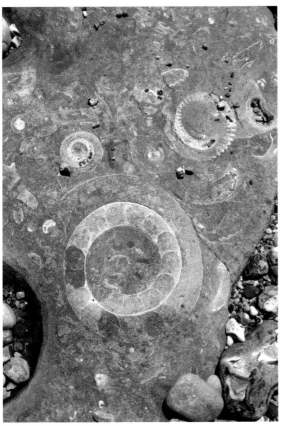

Sturminster Mill
STURMINSTER NEWTON

Sturminster Mill is one of several ancient flour mills built on the River Stour. Still in good working order, the mill runs popular guided tours – though visitors are welcome to roam the mill as they please – and sells freshly ground flour in its gift shop. Peaceful country walks run alongside the river.

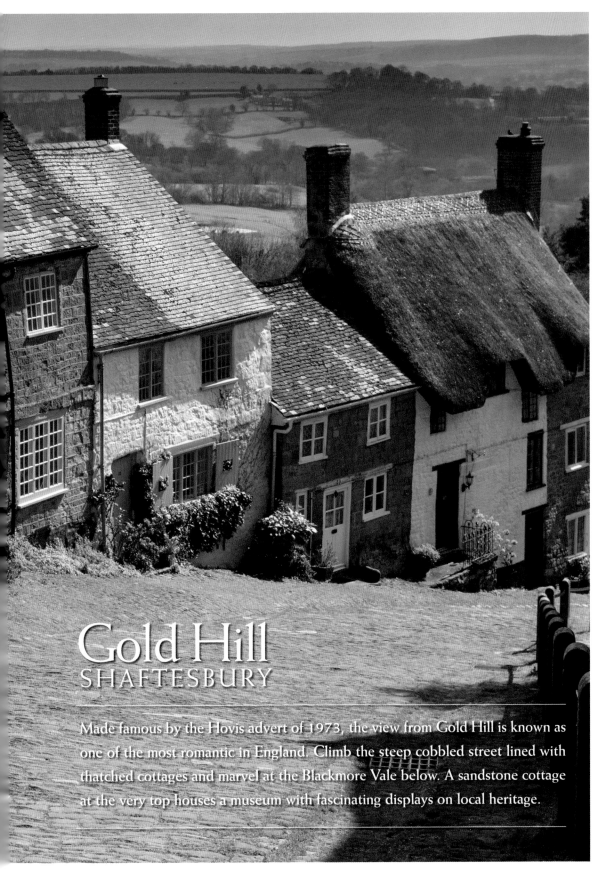

Gold Hill
SHAFTESBURY

Made famous by the Hovis advert of 1973, the view from Gold Hill is known as one of the most romantic in England. Climb the steep cobbled street lined with thatched cottages and marvel at the Blackmore Vale below. A sandstone cottage at the very top houses a museum with fascinating displays on local heritage.

Milton Abbas

Composed of evenly spaced thatched cottages, pubs and tearooms, Milton Abbas is truly picturesque. Footpaths lead from the village to the famous Milton Abbey, set in low wooded hills beside a lake and open to visitors all year round. A unique set of grass steps leads from the gardens up to St Catherine's Chapel.

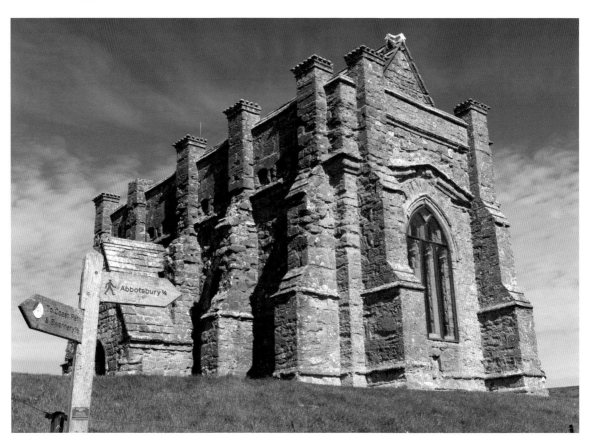

Abbotsbury

Nestled between rolling green hills is the peaceful village of Abbotsbury. Climb to the top of Abbotsbury Hill for a breathtaking view along Chesil Beach to the Isle of Portland. The village's famous Swannery is the only place in the world where visitors can walk among a colony of nesting mute swans.

Wareham

The pretty market town of Wareham lies on the banks of the River Frome. Visitors can board a paddle steamer at the quay for a cruise along the river, or simply relax and watch the boats go by. Walk the town's old Saxon walls or explore the Purbeck area on one of many walking and cycling routes.

Lulworth Cove

Beautiful blue water and calm shingle beaches make Lulworth Cove one of Dorset's most idyllic spots. Head up the cliff paths for the best views of the Cove, and roam east or west along Dorset's Heritage Coast to discover natural bays and fascinating rock formations.

Weymouth

Weymouth's golden beaches are some of the South West's finest, offering traditional seaside activities such as donkey rides, pedal boat hire and Punch and Judy shows. Take the heritage trail around the Old Harbour and discover its rich history, and watch the day's catch come in from one of the many fine pubs and restaurants.

Old Harry Rocks

Carved out over time by the ocean waves, the Old Harry Rocks form one of Dorset's most stunning landmarks. Take a gentle ramble along the coast from Studland to reach these iconic chalk stacks, and enjoy spectacular views over Swanage, Wareham and Bournemouth. Boat trips may also be taken from Poole.

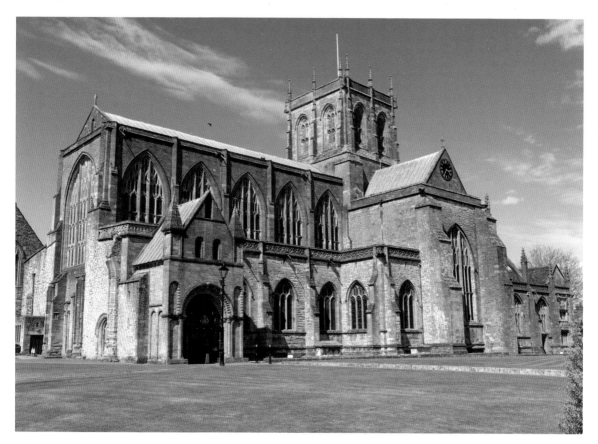

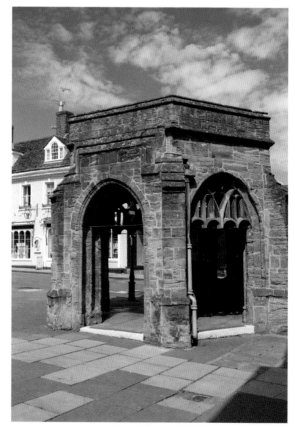

Sherborne

Known for its medieval buildings, magnificent Abbey and two castles, Sherborne is considered one of England's most beautiful towns. Walk the narrow streets and discover antique shops, country pubs and street markets. Walks through the surrounding woodland offer spectacular views over Sherborne Brook and the Yeo Valley.

A TASTE OF DORSET

LYME REGIS · ABBOTSBURY · STURMINSTER NEWTON